Do-whacky-do

Ten baggy clowns were going to town.

One clown said,
"Do-whacky-do,
I can't go with you.
A hen is nesting in my shoe."

Nine baggy clowns were going to town

One clown said,
"Do-whacky-do,
I can't go with you.
I'm off to join a pirate crew."

Eight baggy clowns were going to town.

One clown said,
"Do-whacky-do,
I can't go with you.
I have to paint
my toenails blue."

Seven baggy clowns were going to town.

One clown said,
"Do-whacky-do,
I can't go with you.
I sat in a patch of sticky glue."

Six baggy clowns were going to town.

One clown said,
"Do-whacky-do,
I can't go with you.
I'm taking my crocodile to the zoo."

Five baggy clowns were going to town.

One clown said,
"Do-whacky-do,
I can't go with you.
I'm making a pot of old sock stew."

Four baggy clowns were going to town.

One clown said,
"Do-whacky-do,
I can't go with you.
I'm washing my hair
with green shampoo."

Three baggy clowns were going to town.

One clown said,
"Do-whacky-do,
I can't go with you.
I'm sick with the spotty-dotty flu."

Two baggy clowns were going to town.

One clown said,
"Do-whacky-do,
I can't go with you.
I'm paddling in the bath in my canoe."

One baggy clown was going to town.

One clown said,
"Town isn't fun when there's only one.
So…